HE DISAGREED
WITH SOMETHING
THAT ATE HIM
READING THE LIVING DAYLIGHTS
& LICENCE TO KILL

CARY EDWARDS

CINEPHILES PRESS: FILM READERS

First Published in 2018 by Cinephiles Press

ISBN: 1721810781
ISBN-13: 978-1721810789

Cinephiles Film Readers is a series of titles taking an in-depth look at neglected popular cinema.

The information and ideas set out in this work are those of the author.

Typeset in Palatino Linotype and Gill Sans MT

CONTENTS

Acknowledgement

Much of the research for this work was completed while I was studying the MA Film Studies at The University of East Anglia under the supervision of Professor Yvonne Tasker.

PREFACE

Like many boys who grew up in the 1980s I developed a close relationship with the James Bond films. A perennial fixture on British television, and at the local video rental, the films were ones I watched and re-watched. For many years my favourites were the Roger Moore films, especially *The Spy Who Loved Me, Moonraker* and *Octopussy*. They were light and fun and simple to follow. Around 1989, at the grand age of 10, I found my tastes shifting. This was probably due to the onset of adolescence, but also the effect of the new, dark-gothic, *Batman* film which providing a richer form of escapism than I was used to. This in turn lead me to the comics of Frank Miller and Alan Moore, adding more layers to a character I had once known in Adam West's fabulously campy performance. And into my nascent more cynical world came Timothy Dalton's Bond films.

Dalton's Bond has always been something of a problem. When the films came out, *The Living Daylights* in 1987, *Licence to Kill* in 1989, critical reaction was split. Over the years, spurred on by the lapse in production between *Licence to Kill* and *GoldenEye* in 1995, and Dalton's decision to step away from the role after only two films, there has grown a consensus that the films are failures (particularly

Licence to Kill). Whereas the once reviled *On Her Majesty's Secret Service* (1969), and its star George Lazenby, have been revisited and re-appreciated Dalton's two films remain in the shadows of what came before and after. This was not helped by the dip in box-office that *Licence to Kill* encountered when it was released into the summer of 1989 when Batmania was in full swing.

During that gap of six years I, however, discovered them. They existed only as VHS recordings of edited versions shown on television, but I didn't know any better. They led me to reading all of Fleming's Bond novels (and most of John Gardner's continuation series), revisiting the earlier Connery films and, in a proper sign of teenage obsession, joining the official fan club whose publication *007 Magazine* I devoured ravenously. With no new movies to watch I could only look back and took to memorising as much information as possible. I was a full-blown Bond nerd.

When 1995 rolled around I had become manic in expectation of James Bond's return. I would scour the papers for news, buy any magazine that had Pierce Brosnan on the cover, tape the Tina Turner music video when it was on television and watch it back for clues as to the film's content. This was, of course, before the internet so spoilers were much harder to come by. The novel adaptation was duly absorbed, the television spots and trailers waited for, in a sense of almost religious fervour. And then it debuted, and it was as good as anything I could have hoped for. *GoldenEye* seemed to unify Connery and Moore while the film updated the traditional Cold War setting in a clever and relevant way. Bond was back on top.

Yet something was a bit off. It was during the opening sequence – itself an excellent stream of action and stunts – that it became evident. It was set in 1986. With one stroke Dalton's films were removed. In all probability the date was a reference to when Brosnan was first cast as Bond (only to be denied by his television contract) but it felt like an odd slap in the face to a Dalton fan. As Brosnan's films descended into special effects, thin characterisation and absurdity, Dalton's films grew for me. Here was a version of Bond that seemed closest to Fleming, a more grounded sense of the character to whom killing wasn't a game and the women weren't so disposable. Dalton would never have worn x-ray glasses or driven an invisible car, nor have such a penchant for kissing dead women.

Die Another Day relieved me, after 12 years, of my Bond obsession. Sure, some of the Moore films were bad, in retrospect, but this was worse (not helped by some poor CGI and the stunt casting of Madonna). The producers seemed to know it and, despite healthy box-office, took the radical decision to reboot the series.

So, why return to Dalton now? It's coming up to 30 years since the release of *Licence to Kill* and it remains in many circles an underappreciated film. This book is intended to draw greater critical attention to Dalton's films and revaluate them as a radical attempt to change the Bond series for the better.

In an interview in 2014 Dalton opened up about why he left the series. A man who was never comfortable with global fame and the associated intrusion into his private life discussed how he would have to commit to more films to continue. He was unwilling to make such a commitment: "I thought, *oh, no, that would be the rest of my life. Too much. Too long.* So I respectfully declined" (Meslow, 2014). It occurred to me that Dalton had disagreed with something that ate him.

INTRODUCTION

Timothy Dalton made only two Bond films, *The Living Daylights* (John Glen, 1987) and *Licence to Kill* (John Glen, 1989). The ensuing box-office success of Pierce Brosnan in the role pushed Dalton's brief tenure to the back of the collective consciousness with little critical appreciation outside of some loyal fans. Described by one magazine as "George Lazenby II" (Queenan, 2001) a sense grew that Dalton's films were a little embarrassing, a misstep[1]. Although the films were financially profitable many saw the extended gap in production, between 1989 to 1995, as a direct result of the lack of success of Dalton's films. Indeed, there was a collective sigh of relief in the media when Brosnan was announced as the new Bond in 1994. After all, Brosnan was supposed to have been Bond all along, denied only by a last-minute renewal of a television contract. After Brosnan came Daniel Craig and Bond was reinvented for a new century, becoming as big as in the 1960s. Suddenly taking Bond seriously, popularly and academically, became ok. But within many of the

---

[1] Ironically Lazenby's only Bond film, *On Her Majesty's Secret Service* (Peter R. Hunt, 1969), has undergone a deserved critical re-appreciation and often occurs in top 10 lists of the best Bond films.

analyses Dalton's films remain as missteps, lacking the consideration that the other films have received (a 2018 ranking by *The Guardian* film critic Peter Bradshaw placed them 23rd and 24th, described Dalton as "dull"). This book is intended to repair that and to shed light on a radical moment in one of the longest running and most successful film-franchises. Bond's cultural significance has been well-established, some estimating that half the world's population has seen a Bond film, with the films taking over $2 billion at the American box-office alone. It is within this context that Dalton's films should be understood, but also, they should be seen as existing within a specific socio-political and cinematic context, the latter half of the 1980s. That they are films that, in some ways, broke radically with the established formula is something we will come to.

Chapter One discusses the films as part of the Bond franchise up to that point, with particular focus on how Dalton's two films reinterpreted and transformed the series, breaking with many of the elements that audiences had become familiar with. Several components of the Bond myth were re-written in these films and they will be considered sequentially.

Chapter Two extends beyond the films to consider the contextual influences that account for some of these textual deviations including how Dalton's interpretation relates to Fleming's novels. Chapter Three takes a more detailed and specific look at genre, and how *Licence to Kill* represents a move towards action cinema, and away from the series' traditional adventure elements.

Chapter Four assesses the impact of the films on the box-office and how they relate to the later films in the series, including why the lack of financial success for *Licence to Kill* may have had little to do with the film.

This work is not designed to be a history of the films (Field 2015 covers is all pretty well), more a discussion of the key aspects of Dalton's Bond, what made them different and the contextual factors that helped create them.

Since the mid-1990s there has been a growing critical appreciation of the Bond films and this work is in no way comprehensive of all the publications. It is partly a personal work as well as an academic one, one that I hope will open up Dalton's films for a new audience.

CHAPTER ONE
THE FILMS

In the 25 years between *Dr. No* (Terence Young, 1962) and *The Living Daylights* a series of paradigms were established in the Bond franchise that remained largely consistent, giving the films a secure sense of the "Bondian". Even though:

> the cultural and ideological currency
> of Bond has been changed and
> adapted to changing circumstances
> (Bennett 1987, 1),

the structural elements largely remained the same. The Bond films consistently relied on a small group of character types, plot set-ups and film-makers giving a consistency to the films despite changes in location (including a visit to space). With Dalton's Bonds however, many of these paradigms were broken, with *Licence to Kill* radically re-writing some of them, while simultaneously harking back to Fleming's novels.

Bond is an intertextual creation, a character that exists in and defined by appearances in different media (with film as the most important), and these media help redefine the character in different times for different audiences. But here we shall focus on the film texts themselves and evaluate how Dalton's films stay within, and deviate from, the established franchise parameters.

It is generally agreed that the third film in the series, *Goldfinger* (Guy Hamilton, 1964), established and codified the formula that the subsequent films would follow. Whereas the two previous films, *Dr. No* and *From Russia with Love* (Terence Young, 1963) stayed fairly close to the novels they were based on, *Goldfinger* moved away, developing a more parodic attitude, and the humour the series would become famous for. By *You Only Live Twice* (Lewis Gilbert, 1967) the films had become much less related to Fleming and spectacle was much more emphasised. Compare the novel and film of *You Only Live Twice* and you will find some locations and names in common, and little else. By *The Spy Who Loved Me* (1977), which was also directed by Gilbert, a definite sense of repetition had set in. Writing in American fan magazine *Bondage*, Saul Fisher (1979, 20) recounted 46 similarities between the films, pithily summed up by continuation Bond author Raymond Benson:

> The *Spy Who Loved Me* is basically *You Only Live Twice* using submarines instead of space capsules (1988, 216).

This sense of repetition was not accidental. When writing the screenplay for *You Only Live Twice* Roald

Dahl was given instructions from the producers on how to write the film's women:

> Girl number one is pro-Bond... she is bumped off by the enemy, preferably in Bond's arms... Girl number two is anti-Bond. She works for the enemy... This girl should also be bumped off... Girl number three is violently pro-Bond... she must on no account be killed. Nor must she permit Bond to take any lecherous liberties until the very end of the story... (Quoted in Barnes 1997, 72).

Although not a formula that matches every Bond film, this does apply to *Thunderball* (Terence Young, 1975), *The Spy Who Loved Me* and *Never Say Never Again* (Irvin Kershner, 1983)[2]. Generally, the films pair two women, one of whom sleeps with Bond early in the film and then dies, as seen in *Goldfinger, Diamonds are Forever* (Guy Hamilton, 1971), *The Man with the Golden Gun* (Guy Hamilton, 1974), *Moonraker*

---

[2] I agree with James Chapman that we can consider *Never Say Never Again* to be a "proper" Bond film, despite being made by Taliafilm and not Eon Productions who produce the official films. As Chapman notes it contains "essentially the same ingredients as the Eon films" (1999, 217-218).

16

(Lewis Gilbert, 1979) and *For Your Eyes Only* (John Glen, 1981). The producers clearly retained a tight control on the films.

The gun barrel from The Living Daylights

This sense of repetition extends to other elements of the films and we will looks at them in turn as we consider Dalton's films as part of a series that, until 1989, had only had five different directors and a relatively consistent team behind the scenes led by Albert R. "Cubby" Broccoli (excluding *Never Say Never Again*). This consistency is seen in many of the key signifiers of the series such as the music, the visual style, the gun-barrel opening and other iconography.

The Living Daylights

The New James Bond, Living on the Edge

Three Double-O agents skydive towards Gibraltar on a training mission. One is captured by the SAS. Another is murdered; as he falls to his death the head of the third agent whips round. This is Dalton's Bond, coolly appraising the scene. He sets off in pursuit of the assassin, throwing himself onto the roof of a speeding Land Rover, dangling over the sides as it hurtles down Gibraltar's mountain roads. As the 4x4 breaks through the barriers, and falls towards the Mediterranean, Bond opens his parachute and then glides to a yacht where he interrupts a beautiful woman's phone call. "I need to use your phone" he says as he takes the handset then calls HQ. When proffered a glass of champagne, and the implication of more, she asks for his name. He smiles and utters the immortal line, "Bond, James Bond."

Work before pleasure: Bond calls HQ before being turning his attention to the woman

18

It's a dynamic opening and indicative of the approach Dalton would take in his two films. Whereas Connery first appeared at a gambling table seducing a woman, Lazenby hidden behind hat and glasses (playing on casting an unknown) before dashing into the sea to rescue Tracy and Moore in his Chelsea apartment, caught en flagrante with an Italian agent, Dalton's introduction is less flashy, more direct. He is silent for most of the seven-minute pre-credits sequence, using the action to set the tone of his interpretation. And the woman is second to the action.

Of Dalton's two films *The Living Daylights* hews closest to the established formula, partly due to its development. Until just before production on the film had started the identity of the new James Bond, Roger Moore having retired from the role, remained unknown. The most likely candidate was Pierce Brosnan; indeed, he had been offered the role only to find himself blocked by a last-minute renewal of his *Remington Steele* contract (Barnes 1997, 174). Dalton had been considered as a potential Bond twice before and came back into Broccoli's mind after the prompting of his wife Dana (Broccoli 1998, 280). Such was the speed of his appointment he was introduced to the press on 5th October 1986, after production had started on 29th September. This late appointment clearly influenced the script and tone of the film. The Bond films had evolved to be tailored to the strengths of the incumbent actor. Whereas Connery's films stressed his physicality and ability to ground the ridiculous, Moore's films played on a more distanced and comic persona, something that he had honed on television in *The Saint*. Dalton, however, came to a film which had a generic Bond script. Differences in early drafts of the script written, as had been the previous three films, by Richard Maibaum and Michael G. Wilson, elucidate a shift in tone after Dalton's casting with several humorous scenes being removed (some of the scenes made it to filming before being cut, including one where Bond rides a "magic carpet" over the roofs of Tangier, as seen on the Ultimate Edition DVD).

The film's plot is globetrotting and takes in Bratislava, Vienna, Tangiers and Afghanistan. Some of this is typically Bondian, particularly the Viennese locations, including an opera and the Ferris wheel at the Prater Vienna (a nod to *The Third Man* (Carol Reed, 1949)). Some less so. Bond's visit to Morocco lacks any chance for the bow-tie to be worn. The glamourous backdrop of the Bond films is present but is less dominant than in previous adventures.

A shift was evident not only in what was excluded however, but also in changes in several key areas, particularly Bond's relationship to his superior M. Bennett & Woollacott, in *Bond and Beyond: The Political Career of a Popular Hero*, suggest a psychoanalytic view of the Bond/M relationship:

> [M] functions as the Symbolic Father
> defined, by Lacan, as he who is capable
> of saying "I am who I am"; the source
> of an identity that is complete and full
> in relation to itself, in no need of
> external supports, and in relation to
> which other identities and roles may
> therefore be constructed. M is just that:
> M – a place of pure being, complete
> and final, the originating source of all
> action and centre of meaning (Bennett,
> 1987, 132).

This key relationship, which sees M as an authoritative father and Bond as a rebellious, but ultimately, obeying son[3], is consistent in the Connery and Moore films. The closet Bond ever comes to resisting this relationship, pre-Dalton, is in *On Her Majesty's Secret Service* where Bond plans to resign (although this is scuppered by Miss Moneypenny, who changes his resignation letter to a request to leave).

---

[3] Eco (1966) also sees the relationship in the novels in similar terms.

"If he fires me, I'll thank him for it." Bond's new lack of respect for M.

In *The Living Daylights* we see that this relationship is changing; M has ceased to be the origin of all action. During the narrative Bond denies the instructions of Saunders, M's proxy in Bratislava, disobeys M's orders to ignore Kara as a lead, and chooses to not assassinate General Pushkin. A new set of tensions is revealed in which Bond shows a rebellious streak, telling Saunders that "if he [M] fires me I'll thank him for it", and instructing Moneypenny to keep mission information private. Following the Lacanian structure, it suggests that Bond is beginning to construct his identity apart from the traditional father figure that M represents. When Bond and M meet face to face, in the traditional office setting, the scene is confrontational with Bond describing his decision to not kill Kara as based on instinct, leading M to threaten to remove Bond from the mission with the statement, "I'll recall Double-O-Nine from Istanbul, he follows orders, not instincts." The narrative, of course, backs up Bond's judgements suggesting a reorientation of the relationship, with M losing his status as reliable "source of all action and centre of meaning."

The other major shift from Bondian tradition comes in the relationship between Bond and Kara. Kara differs significantly from most other Bond women as she is not immediately sexually attracted to Bond and her sexual availability is limited by her relationship to one of the films' two villains Georgi Koskov. While not a new idea per se this relationship differs as it lacks the overt sense of abuse evident in Domino and Largo's relationship in *Thunderball* or Andrea and Scaramanga's relationship in *The Man with the Golden Gun*. This leads to Bond standing in a different relationship to her – rather than offering her a way out, a relationship of expedience – theirs is one of romantic seduction seen in extended scenes in Vienna, where Bond challenges her ties to Koskov. Other Bond films contain romantic elements, but generally the women's:

> sexuality was 'free' in the sense that it
> was not tied to marriage, the family or
> domesticity (Bennett 1987, 173).

Kara however, is in a relationship she is happy with (even if it is later to be revealed as a sham) and is seen in an explicitly domestic context; we see her modest apartment after it has been searched by the KGB.

23

Often characterised as a monogamous Bond, Dalton's does sleep with two women (Kara and a woman in the pre-credits sequence), but this is a shift from previous films in which three is the minimum.

Kara in her modest apartment

Beyond her relationship with Bond Kara also differs from her predecessors in the development that her character shows. Instead of being on either side of the good/bad Bond woman divide there are moments of confusion and ambiguity in Kara; in one pivotal scene she betrays Bond to Koskov (by drugging his vodka-martini). This type of betrayal is normally associated with the bad-woman type, such as Fiona Volpe in *Thunderball* or Helga Brandt in *You Only Live Twice*. We also see Kara's character evolve throughout in a way that inverts a common trope in the films. Often the women begin the film strong only to become less capable by the end of the narrative. In *The Spy Who Loved Me* Anya Amasova goes from a competent rival

24

to Bond to a damsel in distress that Bond must rescue – this then confirms Bond's superiority to the women and sees off any challenge to his masculinity. Although Kara does not come to challenge Bond, her development suggests an inversion of this arc. She goes from being a meek and frightened woman to one who rides a horse into a pitch battle between the Russian Army and the Mujahedeen.

Aryan killer Necros, Westpoint dropout Whitaker and fake defector Koskov

The role of the villains in *The Living Daylights* also shows development, again introducing ambiguity into, what had previously been, a largely Manichean[4]

---

[4] A view of the world in which everything is seen in terms of good and evil.

universe. "In Myths and History in the Epic of James Bond", Romano Calisi compares the Bond films to the narrative structure of fairy-tales. Both exist in a world "simplified and rendered transparent" in which there is a "total absence of the problematic" (1966, 81). The plot of *The Living Daylights*, however, involves a level of complexity and ambiguity that was new to the series in that the division between good and evil is no longer simple and obvious. The Russians, who had existed as both villains and allies in several of the previous films[5], are allowed here to exist on either side of the divide with Koskov and Necros on the villainous side, and Pushkin on the heroic. The film's structure includes several reversals; Koskov is introduced as a genuine defector to the West and Pushkin as a psychotic head of the KGB only for their roles to be swapped when it is revealed that Koskov has been playing both Russian and British governments. Similarly, the role of the Mujahideen is complicated; they act heroically, eventually, in supporting Bond but are also part of a heroin smuggling operation (drugs destined for the Western market). Even Saunders, initially depicted as a priggish jobsworth, comes to Bond's aid in Vienna. The one main character who hews closer to the

---

[5] From *The Spy Who Loved Me* to *For Your Eyes Only* there is a complete volte face concerning British/Russian relations.

traditional type is Brad Whitaker, an arms-dealer working with Koskov. He is a rare thing in a Bond film, an American main-villain[6]. The traditional role of the Americans is to support Bond (represented in the films by Felix Leiter, who appears briefly in *The Living Daylights*). Whitaker, who presents himself as a military man with a series of wax-works, of himself dressed as various military commanders including Adolf Hitler and Genghis Kahn, is revealed to be a WestPoint drop-out, another character whose representation shifts.

Villain Whitaker among his waxwork generals

Koskov and Whitaker's combined villainy also shows difference to the previous films in which a single

---

[6] I exclude Mr Big, from *Live and Let Die* (Guy Hamilton, 1973), as he is revealed to be Dr Kananga, from the fictional San Monique.

main villain is supported by henchmen. Koskov and Whitaker share main villain status, crossing the boundaries of the Cold War, both literally and figuratively (through their nationalities). It suggests that old ideas of good and evil are being complicated or dropped entirely, prefiguring the fall of the Berlin Wall two years after the films' release. Koskov's survival of the film, to be repatriated to the USSR by Pushkin for punishment, points to a messier political world where villains aren't always subject to the simple justice of a bullet (or other, more inventive, death). One could imagine Koskov appearing again in a later film using his charm to weasel his way out of prison (perhaps as an oligarch in the post-Cold War Russia?)

Koskov, arrested by the Russians

The film does not, however, avoid all the traditional Bondian trappings. John Barry supplies the music, and cameos, with a-ha's theme very much in the vein of Duran Duran's work for *A View to a Kill*. This plays over titles created by Maurice Binder, responsible for the titles for nearly all the films. Gadgets are well represented in the form of a new Aston Martin DBS (with laser, rockets, skis, after-burner and self-destruct system). Robert Brown (M), Desmond Llewellyn (Q), Geoffrey Keen (Minister for Defence) and Walter Gotell (General Gogol) all reappear from previous films, although Lois Maxwell has been replaced by Caroline Bliss as Moneypenny. Typical scenes also occur: Bond in M's office; Bond visiting Q branch. The stunts are still spectacular, but gone is much of the humour; generally, things are conceived and filmed in a more realistic manner.

Action typical of the franchise: Bond's Aston Martin escapes from an exploding boat shed

The late casting of Dalton is felt in other ways during the film, especially through a tonal inconsistence suggesting elements hanging over from Moore's era

29

that sit uncomfortably with a new, harsher take on the character. One sequence depicts the effect of the war in Afghanistan with Bond and Kara riding through a bombed-out village littered with the bodies of dead Afghans and Russians. Ten minutes, or so, later during the battle scene at the Russian air-base a shower block is demolished revealing soldiers hiding their private parts. The effect is slightly dissonant[7]. With *Licence to Kill* the tone would be consistent.

Licence to Kill

His Bad Side is a Dangerous Place to Be

A small plane is tracked over Miami by an AWACS[8] aircraft. A Latin-American drug lord is in Miami to reclaim his mistress. On the Florida Keys Overseas Highway a Rolls-Royce drives to a wedding. In the back sits a fretting Felix Leiter, friend Sharkey and best-man James Bond. A DEA helicopter descends and soon Leiter, with Bond as an "observer", are in

---

[7] There are some precedents for this. Moore's final three films, *For Your Eyes Only, Octopussy* (John Glen, 1983) and *A View to a Kill* (John Glen, 1985) have similar confusions. In *A View to a Kill* the villain, Max Zorin, drowns and shoots his mine-workers in a film that also plays a Beach Boys song over a skiing sequence.
[8] Airborne Early Warning and Control System.

pursuit. The helicopter lands at a small airfield and a gun-fight ensues. Bond moves from observer to actor. But it's all a distraction. Sanchez, the drugs lord, is escaping in a light aircraft. Bond, Leiter and the DEA pursue in the helicopter. With the line, "Let's go fishing" Bond winches down from the helicopter to the tail of Sanchez' plane, then wraps the steel rope around it. With Sanchez safely in custody, Leiter and Bond sky-dive to the wedding.

Bond in the, relatively, normal world of a friend's wedding

Again, the opening stands out from the other Bonds. Yes, the stunt is spectacular, and the action well filmed, but the context, a friend's wedding, is different. This Bond takes place in a world that could be ours. Bond is amongst friends, jammed into the back of the Rolls, dressed in traditional morning suit. This is Bond away from the glamour of the casinos. There are no women for him to pursue and someone has already used the word "bastard." Things are different. But not in ways everyone appreciated.

In an unofficial companion to the Bond films authors Alan Barnes and Marcus Hearn give a scathing view of *Licence to Kill*'s plot:

> "Drug baron", "raped and killed", "bent on revenge", "private vendetta", "Bond resigns"; do any of these belong in a bonkers James Bond plot? They do not (1997, 189).

The plot itself is, perhaps, the most low-key of all the films. There are only two locations, Miami and the fictional Republic of Isthmus, rather than the globetrotting of most of the series. A traditional casino scene does occur, but interestingly Bond's opponent is Lupe, who becomes his blackjack dealer, rather than the villain himself. A conscious decision has occurred to limit Bond's actions – indeed it is not a traditional "bonkers James Bond plot". Much of what takes place in *Licence to Kill* feels drawn from the real world.

The thematic elements alone mark *Licence to Kill* apart from the preceding films but its differences extend beyond them. For one its title is the first not to be drawn from one of Fleming's novels or short stories. From the very opening, as the white gun barrel moves left to right along the screen, things are different. The opening music, by Michael Kamen rather than series regular John Barry, is more urgent, using high pitched brass and heavy drums instead of the more languid introduction of the Bond theme familiar from previous entries. Kamen's score relies less heavily on the Bond theme than other entries, only being fully used in three action sequences. This contrasts to Barry's approach where the Bond theme would be played:

> when action music would not normally be used, such as shots of Bond walking across an airport concourse or prowling around a hotel room, creating a sense of urgency and movement (Chapman 1999, 62).

But then this film plays out in a different world to the previous films. Early scenes, at Felix Leiter's wedding[9] eschew the typical glamour of the series, placing Bond firmly in an ordinary world, rather than a heightened, more spectacular, version of reality. Traditionally, especially in the 1960s, the use of exotic locations was one of the series' selling points, taking audiences to unfamiliar places. Instead here Bond

---

[9] Played by David Hedison who also played the role in *Live and Let Die.* Until Jeffrey Wright (*Casino Royale, Quantum of Solace*) he was the only actor to play Leiter more than once.

attends an ordinary wedding, a familiar event to most of the audience, and visits the Barrelhead Bar, far from the exclusive glamour of previous adventures.

Changes behind the scenes had also occurred. Production had moved from the traditional home of Pinewood studios to Mexico's Estudios Churubusco (for financial and location reasons), resulting in fewer sets being constructed and locations being repurposed (for examples the Banco de Isthmus is in fact Mexico City's Central Post Office (Glen 2001, 197)). This meant that the grand sets of the type designed by Ken Adam in previous films are largely absent, further grounding the film in reality. There was also a shift in writing responsibilities; Maibaum was forced to stop working on the project due to a strike by The Screenwriters' Guild of America, leaving Wilson to take a greater share of the work than usual (Glen 2001, 189). These are fundamental shifts for such a settled series, ones that part explain the difference in tone that occurs between *The Living Daylights* and *Licence to Kill*.

The growing change in the Bond/M dynamic is taken further here with the characters coming into direct conflict – here Bond's mission is one he takes on himself, against the wishes of his superior. Partly this frees Bond from working within the confines of traditional British hegemony, something that M represents (Bennett 1987, 132). But it also represents a development in Bond's character (which had largely remained unchanged throughout the series). The maiming of Leiter and murder, and possible rape, of Leiter's new wife Della are Bond's motivations, rather than Queen and country. When M meets Bond in Miami the trappings of M's office are avoided[10] he chides Bond for "this personal vendetta that could easily compromise Her Majesty's government." In reaction Bond offers his resignation, but instead is stripped of his licence to kill, effectively delegitimising his actions. As Chapman explains:

> the filmic Bond... had been ironic and slightly rebellious towards his superior, though there had never been any question about his loyalty (1999, 241).

The breakdown of this relationship also has structural effects: the traditional briefing scene is removed: Bond never appears in London; Moneypenny has only a short appearance, and not with Bond. The way M is presented in the film is also different. His appearance in the house in Miami (once

---

[10] M's office often travelled with him, turning up in places as diverse as a submarine, a half sunken RMS Queen Elizabeth and a pyramid.

owned by Ernest Hemingway[11]) draws parallels with the villain Ernst Stavro Blofeld – M is surrounded by cats a symbol inextricably linked to the head of SPECTRE (so much so it was copied in *Never Say Never Again* and re-appeared in *Spectre* (Sam Mendes, 2015)), placing M as an adversary rather than paternal supporter. Later in the film M sends an agent to stop Bond "one way or another." A break in their relationship appears here for the first time, one confirmed when M demands Bond return his Walther PPK.

M confronts Bond, revokes his licence to kill and demands the return of hi Walther PPK

This gun, used in most of the Bond films, was presented to Bond in M's office, in the first film *Dr.*

---

[11] Leading to Bond's quip about "A Farewell to Arms."

No, as a replacement for his previous firearm, a Beretta 418 (with a .25 calibre)[12] described by M's armourer as "nice and light, for a lady's handbag." The Walther PPK symbolises Bond's legitimacy and is a key part of his identity (he is often identified by it) but it also represents his relationship to M the father figure. This is added extra piquancy by the suggestion, from Bennett, that the PPK acts as a phallic symbol, the power given to him by M and part of the symbolic system that has M at its head. Removing this suggests castration, a removal of what Bond "never has of his own but one that he holds conditionally" (Bennett 1987, 133). As Bond escapes with the PPK he claims this symbol for himself, no longer requiring M's approval or endorsement. Later in the film Bond's PPK is removed by Sanchez (who claims Isthmus is a "safe city"), whereupon Bond asks Pam for her gun. She passes him a Beretta 950 Jetfire, a similar shaped .25 calibre pistol to the 418 (which ceased production in 1958). In this Bond symbolically reclaims his original weapon, and thus achieves self-determination. By cutting the umbilical cord to M, Bond symbolically grows up.

---

[12] All weapons details are taken from www.jamesbond.wikia.com and www.imfdb.org

Bond takes the Beretta 950

Turning to the question of the Bond women we see an evolution from Kara in *The Living Daylights*, and a play on an older trope. The two women Bond sleeps with (again he has fewer conquests than typical) are Pam Bouvier and Lupe Lamora. Lupe is a variation on the Bond woman like Domino in *Thunderball* – she is trapped in a relationship with the main villain and sees Bond as a way out. Sanchez treats her sadistically; during the pre-credits sequence he finds her with a lover, who is taken away and killed, and whips her with a sting-ray tail. She becomes a point of competition between Bond and Sanchez, a vehicle for Bond to assert his dominance over the villain alongside the main action. Although Bond does liberate Lupe, by killing Sanchez, he rejects her in the final scene and chooses Pam. Compared to Lupe, Pam represents a paradigm shift in the representation of Bond women and how Bond chooses his women.

Lupe Lamora, a more traditional Bond woman

During the franchise preceding *Licence to Kill* there had been attempts to shift the representation of women with varied results. Bennett argues that as the context of the films changed so the Bond women became more strident, as reflected by Anya in *The Spy Who Loved Me* or Holly Goodhead in *Moonraker*. Both are capable professionals however, as noted above, by the final moments of the film they rely on Bond reasserting his power[13] and any threat to his

---

[13] Bennett suggests "they [the producers] were well aware of the importance of the women's movement and the implication that Bond was unattractive to women because of his outdated sexism. Hence, they saw that while Bond has to fulfil certain sexist expectations revolving around the sexual subjugation of women, it was also important that the girl should be seen to have contemporary resonance with women audiences. Because of this, the Bond production team reworked the theme of the Bond girl's 'out of placeness.' Anya is not 'out of place' in relation to sexuality, nor even 'out of place' in her attempts to do the same job as Bond,

masculinity is removed. With Pam, however, there is no moment where she is depowered or needs to be rescued. Indeed, she seems more aware than Bond at various points; she is negotiating the return of stolen Stinger missiles on behalf of the US State Department, part of a bigger picture that Bond ignores, and she rescues Bond's life on three different occasions. She directly threatens Bond's masculinity; when they first meet she tuts at the size of his gun and reveals, on her lap, a pump-action shotgun. She initiates sexual contact with Bond, to which he retorts "Why don't you wait until you're asked?" This line is reversed in the film's final moments with Bond and Pam kissing suggesting an equality. This is further suggested by their placement in the frame during the kiss, their heads at the same level rather than one above the other[14]. At no point is Pam reinserted in the "patriarchal hierarchy" (Bennett 1987, 194) like most Bond women nor does she need to be rescued at the last moment. Bond rejects Lupe for Pam, a meeting of equals and a new type of relationship in the films.

---

but only in her conviction that she can do better the Bond" (1987, 195).

[14] This is clearly an idea the producers were conscious of, using it for humour when Grace Jones' Mayday reverses the position with Moore's Bond in *A View to a Kill*.

Pam Bouvier a more assertive Bond woman

The main villain's plot, which concerns drug dealing, shows an attempt to reflect more contemporary problems. Disconnected from the Cold War it takes Bond into a new geographical arena: Latin America. This was not a location in Fleming's novels, nor had it particularly featured in the films (it occurs in some scenes in *Moonraker* where the emphasis is on the exotic rather than the everyday). This is important as it shows Bond moving out of the traditional areas of British influence often shown in the films to an area more associated with US foreign policy. Many of the films are set in locations which had been within the British Empire or its sphere of influence (the Caribbean, the Bahamas, Hong Kong, India, etc) or within mainland USA in which Bond acts alongside and with the authorisation of American agencies (often represented by Leiter). Indeed, Anglo-American cooperation is essential to the resolution of various Bond plots, with the US providing support to Bond (*Goldfinger, Thunderball, Diamonds are Forever,*

The Spy Who Loved Me, Moonraker, and *Never Say Never Again* feature this trope). Throughout *Licence to Kill* however, the American authorities are rendered impotent, such as when Leiter is maimed by a shark – amputation being a common symbol of castration. The remaining American characters, excepting Pam, are either unable to help (Agent Hawkins), killed (Sharkey) are on the side of the villain (Killifer, Heller, Milton Krest, Joe Butcher and Truman Lodge). Bond tells Hawkins that "there are other ways" when Hawkins informs Bond the investigation into the attack on Leiter has run aground. Bond's ways will be without official UK or US support in a break from the series' norms.

But what of Bond himself? Dalton builds on the rebelliousness shown in *The Living Daylights* to produce a performance unlike any of his predecessors. Although the theme of revenge had appeared in previous films (*Goldfinger* for example) it was always sublimated to the mission. Indeed, in *For Your Eyes Only* Bond warns Melina Havelock away from such a course of action, and in *The Man with the Golden Gun* Bond informs Scaramanga that "when I kill, it's on the specific orders of my government." Here Bond is given an emotional depth lacking in the previous films – on discovering Della and Leiter's bodies he is visibly shaken. Previous films had existed in a largely black and white world, but there is ambiguity in the one Dalton's Bond inhabits.

Despite the obvious evil that Sanchez represents there are layers of complexity in *Licence to Kill,* even more so than in *The Living Daylights.* At one-point Pam's role is thrown into doubt when Bond spies her meeting with Heller. The role of the British government is questioned when they refuse to intervene in the investigation of Leiter's death (M dismisses this with the line "Leave it to the Americans, it's their mess, let them clear it up") and M later sends an agent to recover Bond. The role of the Hong Kong narcotics agent who has infiltrated Sanchez's organisation creates more ambiguity as does the character of Killifer who betrays Leiter, for a $2 million bribe, but can't stomach watching him half eaten by a shark. Bond himself becomes enmeshed in these issues. His attempt to assassinate Sanchez fails and he destroys Pam's efforts to recover the stolen Stinger missiles; his subsequent capture leads to the death of a British agent and the Hong Kong agents. Taking Sharkey along with him when he goes to infiltrate the Wavecrest leads to his friend's death. Black suggests that Bond emerges in the film as a "certain moral presence against the ambiguities of others" (2001, 154), for instance punishing Heller whereas the State Department might pardon him. In this Bond operates above the conflicted morality of the UK and US governments, but his actions are not without significant cost.

A more casual Bond caught "off-guard" in a normal environment

By avoiding the typical, and multiple, exotic locations of the series *Licence to Kill* also places Bond into a different world, with different rules. As part of this Bond's traditional dress (Saville Row suits and knitted ties) is avoided. The film's costume designer Jodie Tillen's explains that "Bond is caught off guard, so he's not really prepared for this adventure" (Hibben 1989, 61) showing another inconsistency with a series in which Bond has been prepared for almost any situation, no matter how outlandish. It also breaks some of the connections with sophistication and class. As Barnes (1997) suggests, Bond is excessive rather than tasteful in *Licence to Kill*, ordering a whole case of Bollinger champagne, at one point rather than a single bottle (although this could be seen as part of his ruse to infiltrate Sanchez' gang). Much of the humour has been dialled down, removing the detachment that most of the films display. Violence is no longer dismissed with a quip.

Alongside this Bond utters his first swear-words calling Sanchez a "bastard" and later telling another agent to "piss-off." Dalton's Bond broods and looks like he struggles through the film (at the film's action climax he is battered and bruised, his suit torn, a first for the series). This is a Bond haunted by his past; when Della offers to throw her wedding garter to him he refuses remembering his murdered wife. It's this parallel that motivates Bond, Della becoming a proxy Tracy.

Villain Sanchez with diamond collared iguana

The villains are another key element in the film's development of the series. Franz Sanchez represents a much more grounded opponent whose aspirations are financial rather than political. This ordinariness marks him out. When he hosts various Asian drug-dealers he announces, "East meets West, drug dealers of the world unite", demonstrating a rejection of typical Cold War divisions. He also displays charm;

he smiles for the television cameras after his arrest and jokes with his men, displaying some of the verbal wit associated with Bond (for example suggesting some money be laundered after is has been dirtied by Krest's remains). There are hints at a homo-erotic undercurrent in his affection for his young henchman Dario who he nicknames "Manito" (Spanish slang for "little-brother") and "it might be inferred that the villain finds Bond sexually attractive" during the scenes when Bond is staying at Sanchez's villa (Chapman 1999, 244). Certainly, his interest in Lupe seems more as an accessory, like his iguana[15], than as a lover. In general, Bond villains have no character arc, their role is confined to the opposition they present to Bond but here we see how Sanchez develops. As his empire crumbles so does his moral code, based on personal loyalty. Bond's infiltration of Sanchez' organisation is also different, due to the closeness that develops between the two. Bond uses their growing 'friendship' to his advantage. When Sanchez realises the truth, he is personally affected. Physically Sanchez bares similarity to Bond (avoiding the physical deformities of many main villains) which suggests a parallel between the two.

---

[15] Which, in a nod to Blofeld's cat in *Diamonds are Forever*, wears a diamond collar.

Bond and Dario

Dario is also worth discussion as he fails to conform to the characteristics of the typical Bondian henchman. To this point henchmen basically came in two flavours. The first is an extrapolation from Robert Shaw's Red Grant in *From Russia with Love*. A variation on his Aryan styled killer reoccurs in *You Only Live Twice, For Your Eyes Only*, and in Necros in *The Living Daylights*[16]. The other type is a physical grotesque, of which Oddjob (*Goldfinger*) is the first, followed by Tee Hee (*Live and Let Die*), Nick Nack (*The Man with the Golden Gun*) and Jaws (*The Spy Who Loved Me* and *Moonraker*)[17]. Dario is neither of these types. Instead he is represented as a psychopath who, according to the film's UK premier press-book, "is the

---

[16] It would re-appear in the figure of Stamper in *Tomorrow Never Dies* (Roger Spottiswood, 1997).
[17] One could argue that Grace Jones' Mayday fits this in the way the film focusses on her body as a point of otherness and difference.

kind of man that simply takes pleasure in killing." The representation of violence is something else that marks this film apart. Although some elements are brought over from previous films, such as a shark attack, they are constructed in a more explicit fashion showing more blood and mostly lacking the ironic commentary that was used to diffuse such elements. Krest's death, exploded in a decompression chamber, recalls that of Kananga in *Live and Let Die*, but whereas Kananga dies without blood Krest's face expands, explodes and covers the chamber's window with gore. Later when Dario is minced his remains hit the camera lens. Perhaps the most violent death is that of Sanchez himself, with stuntman Paul Weston being set alight in a full-burn, one of the most dangerous stunts that can be performed (*The World of James Bond*).

Sanchez' death: Stuntman Paul Weston performs a full-burn. One of several scenes that were cut to appease censors.

The violence in the film was considered so strong that the British Board of Film Classification (BBFC) demanded cuts to the sequence for the film to secure a 15 classification in the UK (the first, and only, Bond film to be classified as such for its cinema release).

Elements that are more recognizable do exist in *Licence to Kill.* There are gadgets (explosive toothpaste, a signature gun disguised as a camera) but these are largely low key additions. Brown, Bliss and Llewellyn return to their familiar roles (the latter's greatly expanded), and Binder returned for the titles. Sharkey bares comparison to Quarrel from *Dr. No* and Quarrel Jr from *Live and Let Die.* There is humour, particularly in the form of Joe Butcher, and much of the finale takes place in an underground base that duly explodes. But these elements are all twisted to fit this new world.

Despite only making two films the changes discussed above show the radical impact casting Timothy Dalton had on the series. *Licence to Kill,* in particular, broke the mould set down for twenty-seven years in important ways. Relationships were redefined, signifiers were ignored or reinvented, and a more grounded Bond film emerged. Dalton brought layers of self-loathing and anti-authoritarianism to the role at odds to his predecessors. Who knows whether, if he had taken a third shot at Bond, this would have continued?

CHAPTER TWO
CONTEXT

"History is moving pretty quickly these days and the heroes and villains keep on changing places." James Bond, Casino Royale *(Fleming, 1953).*

To consider the causes for this radical change in such an established series leads us to explore three factors that helped push the films in this new direction. Shift in filmmaking personnel and conditions account for some of this, but this is not enough to explain all the changes. Indeed, despite many changes there was continuity, most obviously Broccoli remained on producing duties and Glen as director. Therefore, a more complicated picture needs to be created that takes in cinematic and socio-political contexts, and we will return to the influence of Fleming's novels.

As Chapman explains, over their history "the films have sought to modernise and keep pace with the times" (1999, 64). This change is evident across the films, perhaps most notably in *Live and Let Die, The Man with the Golden Gun* and *Moonraker. Live and Let Die*, released in 1973, was a reaction to the Blaxploitation trend of the time seen in the elements of African-American culture that pervaded the text. *The Man with the Golden Gun*, from 1974, crested the wave of the growing market for Martial Arts films such as *Enter the Dragon* (Robert Clouse, 1973) by including scenes set in a Martial Arts school and in various Asian locations. *Moonraker* (1979) was a direct response to *Star Wars* (George Lucas, 1977), relocating Bond to space – about as far from Fleming's original novels as possible. Fleming's novels were themselves rooted in Cold War tensions, but the filmmakers found themselves adjusting to the shifting geo-political situation. During periods of détente the filmmakers "made efforts to tone down and, in some cases, to eradicate Bond's overt anti-Soviet views" (Bennett 1987, 191). Alongside this was a desire, on behalf of Dalton and the producers, to return Bond to something closer to Fleming's original conception. Post *You Only Live Twice* the films had generally moved away from Fleming, indeed by *Licence to Kill* most of Fleming's novels and short stories had been adapted or used, sometimes in name only. When asked about his inspiration for his performance Dalton answered, "I just went back to the books" (Philip 1992, 132).

Cinematic Context

During the 1980s the Bond films were at a cross-roads. Although still profit making there had been a down turn in box-office grosses from the high point of *Moonraker*, which earned a worldwide gross of $210,308,099, to *A View to a Kill's* gross of $152,627,960[18], with a particularly sharp decrease in the US box office (about $20 million). Other film series had started to break Bond's dominance of the action/adventure market. The Indiana Jones films (*Raiders of the Lost Ark* (1981), *Indiana Jones and the Temple of Doom* (1984) and *Indiana Jones and the Last Crusade* (1989), all directed by Steven Spielberg) were much more successful with *Raiders of the Lost Ark* taking $172 million more than the same year's Bond *For Your Eyes Only*. *For Your Eyes Only* was, itself, an attempt to react to box-office trends, "to make Bond seem a little harder than he had been in previous films" (Glen 2001, 118). The scene in *A View to a Kill* where Zorin kills his own men reflected this, but also demonstrated a confusion as to the direction of the films (the scene was objected to by Moore who stated "That wasn't Bond, those weren't Bond films… You didn't dwell on the blood and the brains" (Barnes 1997, 168)). The finale of *Never Say Never Again*, set in a desert temple location, seemed to be a direct reaction to *Raiders of the Lost Ark,* as did the jungle scenes in *Octopussy.*

Dalton in The Living Daylights: Performing physical action more in tune with 1980s action films. Dalton did as much of the action and stunts as he was allowed.

Alongside the success of Dr Jones was the rise of the multiracial buddy movie. One of the chief progenitors of this was producer Joel Silver who helped launch the cycle with *48 Hours* (Walter Hill, 1982) which paired Nick Nolte and Eddie Murphy. Two franchises produced by Silver, the *Lethal Weapon* and *Die Hard* films, further drove changes in the action genre[19]. A parallel trend in the genre was the development of the spectacularly bodied hero, as embodied by Sylvester Stallone and Arnold Schwarzenegger. All these films shifted the representation of violence in the action genre with

---

[18] Box-Office figures are taken from www.boxofficemofo.com and www.the-numbers.com.

[19] *Lethal Weapon* (Richard Donner, 1987) took $65 million in the US, *Die Hard* (John McTiernan, 1988) took $81 million, well over the Bond film's US grosses at the time.

some, such as *Robocop* (Paul Verhoeven, 1987), pushing the limits of what was considered acceptable. A film such as *Octopussy,* when watched in this context, seems positively tame. So, in one respect it's not surprising that the Bond producers tried to move the Bond films into a more violent mode. Certainly, the casting reflected trends in the wider action genre; John Rhys Davies, Pushkin in *The Living Daylights,* had already appeared in *Raiders of the Lost Ark; Licence to Kill's* Robert Davi (Sanchez) and Grand L. Bush (Hawkins) both appeared in *Die Hard.*

Leiter being fed to the sharks – a more explicit depiction of a Bondian trope

The influence of the emerging trend in action cinema was felt most heavily in *Licence to Kill.* Fred Pfeil, in *White Guys: Studies in Postmodern Domination and Difference,* gives the following description of the narrative formula of the *Die Hard* and *Lethal Weapon* films:

> A white male protagonist, portrayed by an actor of proven sex appeal, triumphs over an evil conspiracy of monstrous proportions by eschewing the support and regulation of inept/craven law-enforcement agencies, ignoring established procedure and running "wild" instead, albeit with the aid of a more domesticated semi-bystanding sidekick (1995, 1).

Licence to Kill happily sits within this formula even imitating the ethnicity of the sidekick in the character of Sharkey (although he is replaced by Q after his death).

Both the protagonists of *Lethal Weapon,* Martin Riggs, and *Die Hard,* John McClane, are beset by domestic problems – Riggs is suicidal following the death of his wife, McClane's marriage is on the rocks. This grounds the heroes in the real world, something *Licence to Kill* imitates in the wedding scenes. Just as Riggs' life is compared to that of his partner Murtaugh, so is Bond's compared to Leiter's. This is then parlayed into Bond's personal vendetta, just as Riggs helps rescue Murtaugh's daughter and McClane rescues his estranged wife. The personal and professional coalesce. This also adds an extra psychological depth to the Bond character that is largely absent from the preceding films. The sadness in Bond's eyes when he finds Della's dead body implies a level of pain Bond is rarely suggested to feel, drawing direct parallels to his own wife's death[20].

The level of physical punishment Bond endures in *Licence to Kill* also reflects the wider trends. By the end of *Die Hard* John McClane is battered and covered in his own blood. This can be seen throughout the action films of the decade, films in which "the boundaries of the body are repeatedly violated" (Tasker 1993, 39).

Bond, bruised and battered, at the end of Licence to Kill

---

[20] Bond's wife Tracy, whom he married in *On Her Majesty's Secret Service*, is referred to only twice before *Licence to Kill*, in *The Spy Who Loved Me* and *For Your Eyes Only*. Neither moment has the dramatic resonance of *Licence to Kill*.

Having the villains motivated by financial gain, rather than world domination or socio/political concerns, is also reflective of the wider genre. Villains such as Hanz Gruber (*Die Hard*[21]) and Arjen Rudd (*Lethal Weapon 2*) only use political motivations as a cover for their financial goals. This linking of criminality to financial markets and mainstream business is shown in *Licence to Kill* by the character of Truman-Lodge who describes drug-operations in the terms of global franchising. The drugs theme is evident in many of the 1980s action films, with the Latin American location imitating films such as *Commando* (Mark L. Lester, 1985), and the Asian ethnicity of the drug dealers Sanchez is courting perhaps reflecting the anxiety of Japanese corporate take-over that pervades *Die Hard* (Pfeil 1995, 20).

Despite the Bond films' distinct identity within action and adventure cinema they continue to reflect current cinematic trends (Daniel Craig's films imitate the *Bourne* franchise in the way the action films are designed and filmed) even though the early Bond films codified many aspects of the genre. With decreasing box-office during the 1980s, is it any

---

[21] Parshall (1991, 140) explains further "The terrorists are a magnified, darker version of the corporate world".

wonder that the Bond producers looked to draw inspiration from contemporary trends?

Political Context

The Bond novels and films have all been rooted to some degree in politics contemporary to their production. As Jeremy Black, in *The Politics of James Bond: From Fleming's Novels to the Big Screen,* explains:

> Both novels and films drew on current fears, but did so in offering a form of escapism from the politics of the age that reassured the public that their future was in good, gentlemanly hands, and that good (us) would always win in the end (2001, xii).

The filmic *Dr. No* reflects paranoia about the Space Race, *Octopussy* about nuclear armament. This is reflected in the flip-flopping between supporting Russia in one film, *The Spy Who Loved Me*, to seeing them as opposition two films later, *For Your Eyes Only*. Fleming's novels were written as Cold War thrillers with Russian agents the main adversaries in many of the adventures, which is seen in Connery's films. As East-West relations warmed in the 1980s so the Bond films had to adapt to this new world.

Despite having a Cold War backdrop *The Living Daylights* complicated simple assumptions of good and bad reflective of the changing times:

> The positive view of Pushkin accorded with Mrs Thatcher's identification of Gorbachev as a Soviet leader with whom she could do business (Black 2001, xii).

The arms deal, hatched by Koskov and Whitaker, offers a direct parallel to the Irangate scandal which was:

> a complex scheme to free hostages held by terrorists by selling arms illegally to Iran, and then secretly diverting the proceeds to provide financial support for the Contra guerrillas in Nicaragua (Chapman 1999, 235).

The film's conspiracy substitutes drugs for hostages, but Whitaker can be seen as a proxy for Colonel Oliver North, the American officer most closely implicated in the scandal. Necros talks of his "brothers struggling for freedom"[22].

Kamran Shah; a Mujahideen leader educated at Cambridge

Much of the action of *The Living Daylights* takes place in Afghanistan in the midst of a complex political conflict, but also a traditional sphere of influence of the British Empire. This location simultaneously shows Britain's decline (it is now in Russia's sphere) and reasserts its power, through Bond's dominance and the figure of Kamran Shah a Mujahideen leader educated at Cambridge. The support shown for the Mujahideen is ironic given more recent events but it's a representation repeated a year later in *Rambo III*

---

[22] The Smiert Spionom element of the plot is a throwback to Fleming's novels in which Smersh (a contraction of Smiert Spionom) were often Bond's adversaries.

(Peter MacDonald, 1988). Humorously the box-office of *Rambo III* may have been adversely affected by the withdrawal of Russian forces from Afghanistan in the week of its cinema release (Tasker 1993, 94).

An Afghan warzone – the harsh reality of geo-political conflict in a Bond film

The politics of *Licence to Kill* are far removed from the Cold War, pre-empting the fall of the Berlin Wall in November 1989. To develop an authentic plot writer Michael G. Wilson:

> embarked on some meticulous research into the way drug barons command respect and loyalty and he uncovered some frightening stories of coercion, intimidation and violence (Glen 2001, 189).

Given Wilson's research it is no surprise that Sanchez, and his fictional realm of the Republic of Isthmus, had a real-world parallel in General Manuel Noriega "whom the Americans were shortly later to 'snatch' and put on trial for conspiring to distribute drugs to the United States" (Chapman 1999, 240).

Black elaborates on Noriega's history and his wider meaning for audiences:

> Noriega, who had dominated Panama since 1983, was accused of corruption and murder in 1987, and the American government unsuccessfully pressed him to resign. The following year, Noriega was indicted, in absentia, in Miami… Sanchez like Noriega has a sinisterly marked face. As far as British viewers were concerned, the Falklands War of 1982 had led to an upsurge in critical coverage of South American military juntas. There was also growing concern that drug dealers were smuggling more South American

drugs into Britain (2001, 151) [23].

Despite the history of Bond opposing Communist Russia *Licence to Kill* has him opposing a Latin-American state that appears to be a right-wing dictatorship in the mould of Panama, further complicating the previously clear politics of the series.

A word on sex is required here due to the reduction of women with whom Bond sleeps in Dalton's film (and a key point of criticism from many critics). Director John Glen directly tied this to the AIDS epidemic of the 1980s:

> This was the 1980s and we couldn't close our eyes to the fact that AIDS had become rampant. It simply wasn't sensible, or fashionable, to depict Bond as a character who slept around (Glen 2001, 177).

---

23 In a classic moment of life imitating art *Licence to Kill* was released before Noriega was 'snatched'. Initial press reaction to the film's plot was incredulous, as Broccoli recalled "They criticised our plot and totally misunderstood our intention to expose top-level corruption in the drug scene. If Noriega had been nailed a year before, the same critics may have accused us of milking the situation" (Broccoli 1998, 295).

The context of AIDS was problematic for a series that had previously been part of the 1960s sexual revolution. The solution was to deepen the women's characters, but this necessitated a reduction in the number of Bond's conquests. Perhaps if the producers hadn't done this, critics would have accused the Bond films of contributing to the crisis. Health concerns aside, Bond was smoking again, something that Dalton fought for rationalising that a man like Bond needed his vices (this resulted in *Licence to Kill* carrying a warning from the US Surgeon General's Office).

A further element of *Licence to Kill* that differs from the previous films is its satiric depiction of television evangelism, represented by Joe Butcher and his Meditation Institute, a conduit used by Sanchez to launder his drug profits – a quite literal interpretation of Marx's condemnation of religion as the "opium of the people."

A film series that had been dominated by the Cold War and simplifying this complex geo-political conflict into Bond's actions had transformed into one in which the storylines were being ripped from the headlines, reframing the Bond films for the threats that had come to exist at the time.

Dalton and Fleming

Benson: How did you prepare yourself for Mr Bond?
Dalton: You know the answer to that, don't you? It's simple. He wrote it. His books gave rise to the first movies. Those movies have gone on for 27 years. He must have done something right. But anyway, beyond that, as an actor, the only way I could approach anything is, I mean I feel my duty as an actor is to work with the author, to reveal the author's intentions. Particularly Casino Royale *which is excellent (Benson 1989, 42).*

It is of great significance that Dalton cites *Casino Royale* as the key inspiration for his performances as Bond. Fleming's debut novel is atypical of the series, although some his later novels have a similar tone. The novel contains a level of "moral meditation and of psychological anger" (Eco 1966, 37) largely absent from the others. By the time Dalton came to play Bond, Fleming's novels had been used up, with elements of his short stories being used as the basis for the early 1980s films[24]. A good amount of Fleming's short of the same name (posthumously published in 1966 as part of the *Octopussy* collection) makes it into *The Living Daylights.*

Bond and Moneypenny – Dalton insisted that Bond smoked in his films, just as he did in the novels

Fleming's short story is transposed from Berlin to Bratislava but the essence of the narrative, in which Bond is sent to kill a sniper who is revealed to be an attractive female cellist, is preserved. This beginning, in which Bond decides against killing her, forms the basis of the film's central narrative as the sniper is revealed to be Kara, girlfriend of villain Koskov. Saunders is based on Captain Sender, a man whose

---

[24] *For Your Eyes Only* is the first of these. *Octopussy* culls from several shorts stories, but *A View to a Kill* bares no relation to its nominal source.

questionable quality we can infer from his education which Fleming disparagingly discusses, part of the rigid social code that Fleming tended to reinforce in his work. The more important borrowing from the source text, however, is Bond's attitude. The moment in which "Bond said wearily "Okay. With any luck it'll cost me my Double-O number"" compares favourably with the filmic dialogue, "if he fires me I'll thank him for it." Black notes this, describing how the film's story "underlines the notion of a spy with a conscience, not an extension of a weapon" and "such an account hitherto had been confined to the printed page" (2001, 83).

For a film that is putatively an original story, with the series' first non-Fleming title, *Licence to Kill* contains a surprising amount of details from Fleming's works (certainly more than supposed adaptations *You Only Live Twice* and *Moonraker*). Leiter's near-death feeding to a shark is straight out of the novel of *Live and Let Die* (1954) as is the grim note "He disagreed with something that ate him" that is attached to Leiter's maimed body. The character of Milton Krest has his origins in Fleming's short *The Hildebrand Rarity* (in the *For Your Eyes Only* collection (1960)) as does Sanchez' use of the Stingray tail as a torture device.

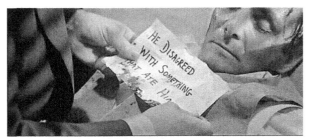
The note left with Leiter's body

Umberto Eco, in his essay "The Narrative Structure of Fleming", deconstructs Fleming's stories into a series of formulae that is evident in each novel. The structure, Eco explains, is patterned around a series of oppositions that "allow a limited number of permutations and reactions" (1966, 39). These oppositions are character based (Bond versus the villain) but also ideological (Anglo-Saxon culture versus non-Anglo-Saxon). The first opposition is essential for understanding how *Licence to Kill* reinvents elements of Fleming that had been largely neglected in the film series. Although the films retained some sense of the opposition of Bond and the villain (particularly though ethnicity and appearance) they generally downplayed the sexual abnormalities that Fleming gave them. As Eco explains, this is key to the villain's otherness:

> [the villain] is asexual or homosexual, or at any rate is not sexually normal (1966, 44).

Sanchez's relationship to both Bond and Dario reflects Fleming's conception, as does his jealous possession and punishment of Lupe. In Fleming's work there is a direct precedent for this in the novel *The Man with the Golden Gun* that implies Scaramanga is attracted to Bond, something that Bond uses when infiltrating his gang[25] which he then destroys from inside (another element that bares comparison to *Licence to Kill*).

Apart from these formal comparisons we can see aspects of Dalton's performance that directly echo Fleming's conception of Bond. The relative sexual restraint Dalton's Bond shows is much closer to the novels in which, as Kinsgley Amis explains, is limited to "almost exactly one girl per excursion abroad, which total he exceeds only once, by one" (1966, 46). The swearing that peppers *Licence to Kill's* screenplay also had precedents in the literary Bond. As he explains to Tanaka, in the novel *You Only Live Twice*, "No self-respecting man could get through the day without his battery of four-letter words to cope with the roughage and let off steam." Certainly, the violence in Dalton's films is close to Fleming. When Sanchez threatens Bond with being minced in his

----

[25] The film adaptation removes this but retains the physical detail of Scaramanga's third nipple.

drugs factory the elaborate tortures Fleming invented are called to mind. Even Bond's personal vendetta can be found in the novels; it is Bond's desire for revenge over the murder of his wife that leads to his reckless determination to kill Blofeld in *You Only Live Twice*. This bares comparison with his fury over Della's death, which harks to his own wife's fate. Other elements that were dialled back in *Licence to Kill*, such as the use of gadgets or the breadth of the villain's plot, are closer to the novels.

Of course, Dalton's films are not adaptations, but they demonstrate a desire to go back to the source of Bond. Many of the initial critics of Dalton's films argued that they had gone too far from their source, that they were too different from the rest of the series. Ironically many of the changes are due as much to Fleming as the filmmakers.

CHAPTER THREE
LICENCE TO KILL & GENRE

Bond: I help people with problems.
Sanchez: Problem solver.
*Bond: More of a problem **eliminator**.*

What genre are the Bond films? It sounds like an obvious question, but it's an important one. They sit in the broad category of action-adventure cinema but, traditionally, with a stress placed more on adventure than action.

The term action-adventure can be traced back to 1927 in a description of the Douglas Fairbanks film *The Gaucho* (F. Richard Jones) (Neale 2000, 55). The early films sprang from romance literature (the chivalric kind) and that basic structure of a knight rescuing a damsel can be seen in many of Fleming's works, something he acknowledged in the novel *You Only Live Twice* when Tiger asks Bond (in reference to Blofeld's hideout) to "enter this Castle of Death and slay the Dragon within". Alongside this Fleming stirred in the influences of his own, very English, upper class upbringing, his military experiences and journalistic globetrotting with a more American inspired hard-boiled approach to violence (it's of note that Raymond Chandler was a Bond fan). It makes the novels rather odd hybrids for the time, and this extends to the films, although in slightly different ways. Although nominally British they were brought to the screen by an American, Broccoli, and a Canadian, Harry Saltzman (for the first nine films). For the first eighteen films the directors were British, but the main screenwriter, Richard Maibaum, was American. It makes them transatlantic productions reflecting certain British values, wrapped up in a level of Hollywood style production unusual for British films of the time.

In many ways they redefined screen violence and action, while retaining a sense of the adventure film's lone hero by suturing some of Fleming's more outré ideas (villains with metal hands, killer bowler hats, etc) to a globetrotting exoticism. As the films developed they largely moved away from their literary sources and introduced more of what the audience responded to: humour, gadgets and spectacular action. Although the first two Bond films, *Dr. No* and *From Russia with Love* are, arguably, espionage thrillers by *Goldfinger* they had become action-adventure films proper.

Thomas Sobchack explains traditional action-adventure film narratives:

> a protagonist either has or develops
> great and special skills and overcomes
> insurmountable obstacles in
> extraordinary situations to

successfully achieve some desired goal, usually the restitution of order to the world invoked by the narrative. The protagonists confront the human, natural, or supernatural powers that have improperly assumed control over the world and eventually defeat them (1998, 9).

It's a formula that fits the Bond films post *Goldfinger* well. Bond uses his own abilities, with some help from Q, Leiter, etc., to avert a threat that has often global implications. It worked spectacularly. Adjusted for inflation *Thunderball* is still the most successful of the films at the US box-office. This balance, of traditional adventure with spectacular, and novel, action elements, was key to the films' success. It was a formula however that started to suffer as the 1960s came to an end.

By the early 1970s the modern action film developed out of the ashes of the Western. Films such as *Coogan's Bluff* (Don Sigel, 1968), *Bullitt* (Peter Yates, 1968), *Dirty Harry* (Don Siegel, 1971) and *The French Connection* (John Frankenheimer, 1971) codified the modern action movie and the Bond films struggled to respond, with *The Man with the Golden Gun* suffering at the box-office. Indeed, after the box-office high point of *You Only Live Twice* the films had become rather schizophrenic as the filmmakers struggled to move Bond forward against the growing competition. The producers' solution to *The Man with the Golden Gun's* poor box-office, was to create a kind of greatest hits package in *The Spy Who Loved Me*, which dialled back on the action and instead worked more as pure adventure. *Moonraker*, which followed, has an almost identical plot but swapped the ocean for space. Sensing diminishing returns (after all, where do you go after space?) *For Your Eyes Only* tried to bring in more hard-edged action scenes and a more grounded espionage plot with mixed results. Ironically a more traditional adventure, *Raiders of the Lost Ark*, would dominate at the box office in 1981.

The struggles to compete with developments in the action film was, in many senses, doomed. Although sharing aspects with action-adventure the pure action film is fundamentally different. As O'Brien explains, the action film:

> is built around a three-act structure centred on survival, resistance and revenge. It is a narrative of social and personal redemption in which the act of will is embodied in the physical body of the hero – tested, traumatised and triumphant (2012, 14).

The Bond films, until *Licence to Kill,* struggle to fit into this formula. The key aspect they lack is revenge. Bond's motivation, until 1989, was largely Queen and

Country. Even the death of his wife, at the end of *On Her Majesty's Secret Service,* is mostly ignored; in the subsequent film, *Diamonds are Forever,* a personal grudge against Blofeld is suggested early on, but quickly forgotten. This personal motivation is, however, the core of the modern action film and by centring the plot of *Licence to Kill* on this moved the Bond films away from the action-adventure hybrid to be firmly in the action genre. This focus strips away many of the adventure trappings of the previous films (such as the globetrotting), added the "tested, traumatised" body of the hero (as discussed in the previous chapter) and reoriented it towards a new audience.

During the 1960s the Bond films had managed a broad audience appeal, embracing men, women and families. During the 1970s however, there was a general reorientation in Hollywood towards a younger, male, target audience (see Krämer (1999) for more on why this happened). As mainstream Hollywood pushed for that audience, hence the predomination of action films in the 1980s and 1990s, perhaps alienating women from attending the cinema, the Bond films began to look more out of step with trends. [26] When John Glen took over directing duties of the Bond films, with *For Your Eyes Only*, there was a clear attempt to shift towards the inclusion of more direct action elements, but this is contained within the retaining of an appeal to the traditional audience (hence the lack of blood, swearing or explicit sex). By shifting *Licence to Kill* firmly into action, rather than action-adventure, the traditional audience was abandoned but a newer audience, who may have responded more positively to the film, wasn't found. Issuing its first swear word in the first few minutes *Licence to Kill* must have been a dissonant experience for a traditional Bond fan, but those audiences who craved action may have avoided it because it *was* a Bond film, something they associated with the 'safer' films of the past.

GoldenEye marked a return to the more adventure-based style of Bond film, reinstating the globetrotting and global stakes with Bond's personal vendetta against ex-006 Alec Trevelyan becoming a sub-plot rather than main motivation. This tendency continued across Brosnan's films with aspects of

---

[26] This of course becomes a self-fulfilling prophecy – the more Hollywood believes that one audience is dominant the more it makes product for that audience, thus encouraging that audience and discouraging others.

Bond's personal life providing texture, but never the focus of the films.

Ironically, and in the wake of the Bourne films (especially *The Bourne Supremacy* (Paul Greengrass, 2004)), the Bond series has shifted towards embracing more action orientated narratives with personal vengeance being a core aspect of *Quantum of Solace, Skyfall* and *Spectre.* With the reboot however, placing Bond as a newly qualified Double-O agent in *Casino Royale,* a cleaner break with the franchise was made. *Licence to Kill* remains in continuity with the previous Bonds (as much as they have continuity), lacking the new beginning that Craig's films have benefitted from.

The importance of genre to a film's perceived success can't be overstated. It is something that audiences are implicitly aware of, and producers embrace in the marketing of their product. It is key in the audience's choice of film. In *Visible Fictions* John Ellis discusses the concept of "narrative image":

> An idea of a film [that] is widely circulated and promoted, an idea which can be called the "narrative image" of the film, the cinema industry's anticipatory reply to the question "What is this film like?" If anything is bought at the box office

> that is already known by the audience,
> it is the narrative image (1992, 30).

Re-watching the theatrical trailer for *Licence to Kill* a confusion can be seen. It opens with Leiter being fed to the shark, before cutting to Dalton, gun in hand, and the word Bond superimposed over the image. It's hard hitting, but later in the trailer the traditional Bond theme begins playing over a montage of action beats. Lip-service is paid to the film's difference to the series, but the traditional music suggests otherwise. Compare this to the trailer for *The Living Daylights* which is much more in line with Bondian tradition (showing the gun-barrel, gadgets and action), including the voice over line "Where he goes, *adventure* follows." The marketing for *Licence to Kill* is not confident enough in the film's differences to the series and the move towards action, but neither does it pull the other way and stress the links to the series. Its narrative image was confused, its genre muddled.

CHAPTER FOUR
LEGACY

His [Dalton's Bond] had his virtues. Less overtly macho than Connery, less robotically resourceful than the elegant but occasionally animatronic Brosnan, Dalton transformed the mythic James Bond into something more human. And after the carnage visited in the saga by the twitish Moore, Dalton was a breath of fresh air, if nothing else (Queenan 2001, 52).

Assessing the impact of Dalton's two films is difficult and complicated by the gap in production between *Licence to Kill* and *GoldenEye* (Martin Campbell, 1995). The financial success of Dalton's films was mixed. *The Living Daylights* grossed $191 million worldwide (up from *A View to a Kill's* $152 million) but *Licence to Kill* a disappointing $156 million, nearly $40 million less than its predecessor. The idea that Dalton's films were failures was given further credence by Brosnan's debut success in *GoldenEye* which grossed over $356 million. When ticket sales were considered, rather than grosses, *Licence to Kill* gave the series its lowest viewing figures since 1974's *The Man with the Golden Gun.*

Critically however the picture was more complex. In response to *The Living Daylights* Victoria Mather, in *The Daily Telegraph*, suggested that "Dalton has restored a vital element to OO7 – the very best of British, the amateur gentleman who is better than any professional" (1987). *The Washington Post* approved and suggested that "Dalton, no waffler, develops the best Bond ever" (Kempsley 1987). *Monthly Film Bulletin* described it as "exhilarating" and "spectacular" (1987, 244) and *Variety* suggested it "will be tough to top… everyone seemed up for this one and it shows" (quoted in Lisa 1992, 131). Many of the Bond fan community were also positive concerning *The Living Daylights.* Kevin Harper, in *OO7 Magazine*, suggesting it "marks the return to the screen of the REAL James Bond" (1998, 45). If anything, the success of *The Living Daylights,* and of Dalton, pushed the filmmakers into making *Licence to Kill* a more hard-edged film. Dalton's debut had been promoted with the taglines, "The Most Dangerous Bond Ever" and "The New James Bond, Living on the Edge." The box-office success was affirmation of this approach. Success, however, would not carry over easily.

Licence to Kill disappointed at the box office and there are multiple reasons why. We could point to the paradigm and genre breaks the film offers. Each Bond film walks on a tightrope, balancing innovation and tradition; had *Licence to Kill* simply gone too far?

The truth is more complicated. Screen tests had gone well. Rated "outstanding" by test audiences it had "received the highest [rated] test-screening of any Bond film" (Glen 2001, 208). This did not convert, however, to ticket sales. Bond films had long had summer releases but 1989 was a more congested year than others. Released on 13th June *Licence to Kill* was pitched into the middle of a box office battle between *Indiana Jones and the Last Crusade*, *Lethal Weapon 2* (Richard Donner), *Ghostbusters II* (Ivan Reitman), *Star Trek V: The Final Frontier* (William Shatner) and the all-conquering box-office giant *Batman* (Tim Burton). Both *Licence to Kill* and *Star Trek V* suffered despite being part of successful, well-liked, franchises.

Cover for the UK Premier Press Book

The marketing campaign for *Licence to Kill* also caused issues and implied production problems. Originally the film was to be titled *Licence Revoked*, a title more indicative of the film's narrative, but this was changed when market research suggested American audiences may not understand the word "revoked" or would associate the phrase with their driving licences[27].

This resulted in an expensive, and striking, advertising campaign being ditched. The discarded campaign strongly communicated the film's ties to the series, but also its narrative innovations. "Dismissed, Disgraced, Dishonoured, Deadly" read one. "You're Looking At The World's Most Wanted Man" read another (Rebello 1989, 15). The artwork, some of which was done by Bob Peak a veteran of several blockbusters including *The Spy Who Loved Me*, was striking and emphasised Dalton in action. MGM/UA's replacement campaign was completed in-house and lacked inspiration, the US poster, in particular, being a drab affair of cut and paste images. As screenwriter William Goldman suggests the effect

---

27 Accounts differ on this. Glen (2001, 206) and Barnes (1997, 185) suggest it was the meaning. Lisa (1992, 233) suggested the confusion with a driving licence. It may also have been confused with John Gardner's official Bond continuation novel *Licence Renewed* (1981).

of these changes can be a major signal to the press and public, "changing the ads, a sure sign a picture is in trouble" (1996, 71). This was further complicated when an issue with the spelling of the new title arose: either the US *License* or the UK *Licence*[28]. As Bond was British the latter spelling was chosen. Director Glen suggested that the film was underpromoted, "I personally saw little more than a television commercial and some posters in bus stops" (2001, 208). In the summer of Batmania, *Licence to Kill* got lost.

Mixed reviews cannot have helped either. Some were lavish in their praise, such as Michael Wilmington in *The Los Angeles Times*:

> *Licence to Kill* is probably one of the five or six best of Bond. This is a guilt-edged Bond; there's a core of darkness and pain in the glittery world exploding around it (quoted in Lisa 1992).

Derek Malcolm, writing in *Midweek*, was less positive, describing it as "average" (quoted in Barnes 1997).

---

[28] Different poster concepts have different spellings.

Nigel Andrews of *The Financial Times* felt it had moved too far from the established formula:

> Rather than raising the temperature the movie's much publicised (though hardly shocking) violence, demoted the film to the dominion of the ordinary. Thick-eared action films we can get anywhere (quoted in Barnes 1997).

This split characterised the reactions to the film; either people were on board with the changes or they rejected them as too radical[29].

When Bond returned in 1995, in *GoldenEye,* the distance from *Licence to Kill* was stark. Dalton was gone and so were the innovations that marked his films. *GoldenEye's* advertising campaign stressed a return to traditional Bondian elements with one tag-line reading "You Know the Name, You Know the Number". The teaser trailer opened with the line, "It's a new world, with new enemies and new threats. But you can still depend on one man" with Brosnan shooting the final letters into 007 and then

---

[29] In the UK this was further complicated by the 15 Certificate from the BBFC, excluding younger audiences from the film and perhaps alienating those more used to Moore's more sedate entries.

approaching the camera to say, "You were expecting someone else?" (suggestive of the break with Dalton). Back was the bow-tie and tuxedo that vanished from the *Licence to Kill* promotion and Bond was up to three sexual conquests. Although M was now female, played by Judi Dench, their relationship was closer to that between Connery and Bernard Lee – some chiding, followed by parental affection. Critics and audience largely agreed that the film was a return to form. Dalton's tenure in the role could be forgotten. Six years was a long time.

Signed photos of Dalton and Brosnan typical of their different approaches to Bond

Retrospectively the six-year gap between Bonds contributed to the idea that Dalton's films were failures, his lack of a third appearance seemingly confirming this. The true picture however is more complicated. An extensive discussion of the legal issues that kept Bond from the screen are unnecessary here, but it clearly took its toll on the filmmakers. Michael G. Wilson (now producer of the Bond films) described the complex legal fight over rights with MGM/UA's owner Giancarlo Peretti, in that the producers "had to fight our way through that [the legal issues], which took three years" (Westbrook, 1995, 88). Finally, free of the legal hassles which had prevented the development of a third Dalton Bond (ideas for which can be found online) and with Broccoli in ill health, Eon productions gathered its forces to make a new Bond film. Screenwriter Michael France was employed on the assumption that Dalton would return[30]. He explained:

> It was sort of generally assumed that
> it would be Tim... I tried to write it
> with him in mind (Barnes 1997, 192).

Indeed, elements of Dalton's Bond can be seen in *GoldenEye*, especially in the attempts to give Bond some psychological depth. When villain Trevelyan asks Bond whether "All those martini's silence the screams of the men you've killed?" some of Dalton's

---

[30] Broccoli pushed for Dalton to return, despite objections from the Fleming estate's representative Kenneth Maidment who thought Dalton's portrayal was the main cause of falling revenue (Hastings 2006).

angst comes to mind as does the personal relationship between both – although, unlike *Licence to* Kill, the mission manages to coalesce a personal revenge with national duty. Generally, the women have more active roles in the film and making M a woman, who chides Bond for being a "sexist, misogynist, dinosaur," adds to this. However, by entering a dialogue about Bond's values the film creates an ironic distance that allows Bond's excesses to be indulged (excepting the smoking) as opposed to the attempts to change them or ground them as per Dalton's films. The more aggressive and physical action beats also recall Dalton's two films.

Brosnan's Bond is also more traditional. He retains his suit for the majority of the running time, eschewing the more casual approach of Dalton. The Aston Martin DB5 was back (the same model as seen in *Goldfinger* and *Thunderball*) tying him to Connery and helping Bond crest a wave of 1960s nostalgia evident in the 1990s (alongside Bond other 1960s properties were revived in the decade with mixed results. These include *Mission: Impossible* (Brian DePalma, 1996), *The Saint* (Philip Noyce, 1997) and *The Avengers* (Jeremiah S. Chechik, 1998)). Brosnan himself seemed born to play Bond, regularly telling interviewers of one of his first visits to the cinema was to see *Goldfinger* in 1964. Brosnan himself was seen more as a light romantic lead, his image formed in the *Remington Steele* television series and in films such as

Mrs Doubtfire (Chris Columbus, 1993), a similar background to Moore. Dalton, however, was an actor more known for his theatre work than his occasional film appearances. Indeed, the type of actor Dalton represented was more often seen as the villain, such as Alan Rickman in *Die Hard,* Joss Ackland in *Lethal Weapon 2* or fellow Welshman Anthony Hopkins in *The Silence of the Lambs* (Jonathan Demme, 1991). This is something Dalton would later play up to in *The Rocketeer* (Joe Johnston, 1991) and *Hot Fuzz* (Edgar Wright, 2007), both films that showcased Dalton's ability to handle humour, something he was often accused of lacking.

Brosnan's other Bond films, *Tomorrow Never Dies, The World is Not Enough* (Michael Apted, 1999) and *Die Another Day* (Lee Tamahori, 2002) continued to offer some glimpses into Bond's psychology, especially in his relationship to women, but it was surrounded by the sort of over-the-top spectacle Dalton's films avoided. The stakes increased until Brosnan's Bond was preventing all-out war between North and South Korea. They were a long way from *Licence to Kill's* attempt at placing Bond into the real world.

AFTERWORD

Despite good box-office returns for *Die Another Day*, $431 million worldwide against a $142 million budget, Bond's producers Michael G. Wilson and Barbara Broccoli (step-son and daughter of Albert Broccoli) decided to cut ties with Brosnan. Sensing a shift in the nature of action movies and perhaps suspecting that they could go no further with the escalating stakes of the films a radical decision was taken; reboot the series, cutting all ties with what went before. Having finally attained the rights to Fleming's debut novel they cast Daniel Craig as James Bond in *Casino Royale*[31]. Avoiding the CGI excesses of the previous film this Bond seemed to exist in the real world, his relationship to his superiors fractious at best. The gadgets were stripped back, and Bond was allowed to fall in love, suggesting an emotional depth. He also suffered physically, particularly in one scene, drawn straight from Fleming, which had many male audience members crossing their legs in sympathy. Much of it was oddly familiar to a Dalton fan.

---

[31] A previous adaptation, in 1967, was a spoof of the franchise, with no relationship to the Eon films.

Along with a record number of viewers, box-office totalling over $594 million, I sat in the dark of the cinema and watched transfixed as Craig debuted his tougher, more physical Bond. It was a shot in the arm to a franchise that I had given up on. It was not to last. *Quantum of Solace* (Marc Foster, 2008) followed. A problematic production process clearly showed through in a disjointed film with some good action scenes but a lack of narrative drive. *Skyfall* (Sam Mendes, 2012) came next and I found myself out of step with nearly the whole cinema going world. A huge success, and the first Bond to gross over a $1 billion, I found it non-sensical, the action poorly coordinated and the film's treatment of women nauseating[32]. *Spectre* was simply dull.

My love of Bond films had been a long odyssey. From childhood wonder, to adolescent obsession and then to adult indifference. But then I'm nearly 40 and I'm not sure these films are being made for me anymore.

Re-watching Dalton's films, and revisiting thoughts I had at university nearly 18 years ago, has brought back the pleasure I found in them. They are not perfect and certainly the pacing is slower than I

---

[32] This may be my age or being a father to a daughter, but I found the representation of the women in *Skyfall* to be highly problematic, particularly the character of Séverine.

remember. There are moments of poor back-projection and the editing could be tighter. The action and stunts however, particularly in *Licence to Kill*, are excellent. And Dalton remains my favourite Bond, the only one, I believe, to capture the true nature of Fleming's creation as it was on the page, the mixture of cynicism and ennui Fleming named *accidie*. Fleming wrote about a professional killer who coped with life through a mixture of cigarettes, alcohol and love affairs. It was not an ironic creation, more a heightened version of Fleming's own identity and fantasies. *Licence to Kill* was the last Bond film in which "Cubby" Broccoli was actively involved (ill-health preventing him from taking much of a role in the production of *GoldenEye*) and as I watch it again it offers closure to the original series of films: a Bond who no-longer needs M or Her Majesty's government, who has come to terms with his wife's death and can fall in love with a woman who is as strong as he is, one that doesn't need rescuing.

The two films are, clearly, not to everyone's tastes, but I they are not failures; they're an attempt to transform what the cinematic idea of James Bond was. They're Bond films for adults. And I am not alone. In the 31 years since *The Living Daylights* more and more fans have discovered Dalton's Bond and come to appreciate what he and the producers were trying to do. In an age of cookie-cutter blockbusters firmly aimed at a PG-13 audience, I look back with surprise that anyone was that brave.

PLOT SYNOPSES

The Living Daylights

While on a training mission in Gibraltar James Bond chases, then kills, an assassin who had murdered a fellow Double-O agent. The action then moves to Bratislava, Czechoslovakia, where Bond is tasked with overseeing the defection of a Russian General, Georgi Koskov. Bond chooses against killing a supposed KGB assassin, the cellist Kara Milovy.

Bond returns to the UK and is tasked with assassinating General Pushkin, based on information from Koskov. Bond is dubious in accepting the mission and, secretly, arranges to find Kara. He learns she is Koskov's girlfriend and was going to fire blanks at Koskov to make his defection seem real. Back in the UK Koskov's safehouse is invaded by killer Necros, and Koskov is kidnapped. Bond finds Kara under KGB surveillance. He convinces her he is working with Koskov and escapes with her across the border to Austria, despite the attentions of the local military.

In Vienna Bond is informed that Koskov is in Tangiers with Brad Whitaker, an arms dealer. The agent who informs Bond is murdered by Necros, leading Bond to angrily pursue his mission towards Pushkin. In Tangiers Bond agrees not to kill Pushkin, in an attempt to learn of Koskov's relationship with

Whitaker. Bond fakes Pushkin's death and escapes only to be drugged by Kara who has contacted Koskov on her own. Bond and Kara are taken by Koskov to Afghanistan where it is revealed that money given by Russia to buy arms from Whitaker is instead being used to buy opium which will then be sold for a profit. Bond, and the now betrayed Kara, escape only to be captured by Kamran Shah and the local Mujahedeen. Bond asks for help and despite resisting Shah gives Bond explosives. After the opium deal is complete Bond is trapped in a Russian truck; Kara and the Mujahedeen take pursuit. A battle ensues in which Bond escapes, with Kara, in a plane loaded with opium.

After several near-death moments the film moves back to Tangier where Bond confronts and kills Whitaker. Pushkin arrives to take Koskov back to Russia.

In London Kara gives a command performance on the cello. Back stage Bond waits for her.

Licence to Kill

While at Felix Leiter's wedding in Miami Bond helps Leiter and the DEA capture a Latin American drugs baron, Franz Sanchez.

Sanchez bribes a DEA agent, Killifer, with $2 million to help him escape. Sanchez has Leiter kidnapped and his new bride killed. As a warning to others Sanchez feeds Leiter to a great-white shark but does not let him die. Hearing that Sanchez has escaped Bond returns to Leiter's house to find the bride dead and Leiter half-eaten.

As both British and American authorities refuse to pursue Sanchez, who is now back in the Republic of Isthmus, Bond sets out on his own, following a lead to the Wavekrest, a yacht owned by a Sanchez' affiliate Milton Krest. Here he speaks to Sanchez' girlfriend Lupe. Bond hijacks a drugs deal, flying away in a plane containing $5 million.

Bond meets Pam Bouvier, an associate of Leiter and former pilot, in a bar. After a fight with Sanchez' henchman Dario, the two escape and agree to work together.

Flying into Isthmus Bond pretends to be a gun for hire. He becomes friendly with Sanchez and starts to persuade him that there may be disloyalty in his organisation.

Bond attempts to assassinate Sanchez but is interrupted by Hong Kong narcotics agents, who are investigating Sanchez. Bond is captured and about to be repatriated to the UK when Heller, Sanchez' general, attacks the Hong Kong agents' house killing them. Bond is rescued and gets closer to Sanchez. While at Sanchez' villa Bond sleeps with Lupe; she thinks he can help her escape.

The Wavekrest arrives in Isthmus and Bond arranges for the $5 million to be hidden aboard, with the help of Pam and Q, recently arrived from London. Sanchez finds the money and kills Krest.

Sanchez takes some investors to see his drugs distribution centre, and Bond joins the group. Here he is recognised by Dario. In trying to escape Bond starts a fire but is captured. As Dario is about to kill Bond, Pam intervenes. Bond then chases Sanchez' drugs smuggling trucks, destroying them and killing Sanchez.

At a party Bond rejects Lupe and, having leapt off a balcony into a pool, reunites with Pam.

KEY PRODUCTION CREDITS

The Living Daylights

Directed by John Glen.

Produced by Albert R. Broccoli & Michael G. Wilson

Written by Richard Maibaum & Michael G. Wilson

Adapted from the short story *The Living Daylights* by Ian Fleming.

Key Cast

Timothy Dalton as James Bond

Maryam d'Abo as Kara Milovy

Jeroen Krabbé as General Georgi Koskov

Joe Don Baker as Brad Whitaker

Art Malik as Kamran Shah

Music by John Barry

Title Song performed by A-h*a*

Cinematography by Alec Mills

Edited by John Grover & Peter Davies

Production Companies: Eon Productions/United Artists

Distributed by MGM/UA Communications Co in the USA, United International Pictures worldwide.

Premier: 29 June 1987, London

Running time: 131 minutes approx.

Licence to Kill

Directed by John Glen
Produced by Albert R. Broccoli & Michael G. Wilson
Written by Michael G. Wilson & Richard Maibaum
Based on James Bond created by Ian Fleming
Key Cast:
Timothy Dalton as James Bond
Carey Lowell as Pam Bouvier
Robert Davi as Franz Sanchez
Talisa Soto as Lupe Lamora
Anthony Zerbe as Milton Krest
Frank McRae as Sharkey
Everett McGill as Killifer
Wayne Newton as Professor Joe Butcher
Benicio del Toro as Dario
Anthony Starke as Truman-Lodge
Music by Michael Kamen
Title Song performed by Gladys Knight
Cinematography by Alec Mills
Edited by John Grover
Production Companies: Eon Productions & United Artists
Distributed by MGM/UA Communications Co. in the
USA and United International Pictures worldwide.
Premier: 13 June 1989, London.
Running Time: 133 minutes approx..

BIBLIOGRAPHY

Amis, Kingsley (1966) *The James Bond Dossier*. London:
Pan.

Barnes, Alan and Hearn, Marcus (1997) *Kiss, Kiss, Bang,
Bang: The Unofficial James Bond Film Companion*. London:
B.T. Batsford.

Bennett, Tony and Woollacott, Janet (1987) *Bond and
Beyond: The Political Career of a Popular Hero.* London:
MacMillan Education Ltd.

Benson, Raymond (1988) *The James Bond Bedside
Companion.* London: Boxtree.

Benson, Raymond (1989) Poetic Licence. *OO7 Magazine*.
38, 38-45.

Black, Jeremy (2001) *The Politics of James Bond: From
Fleming's Novels to the Big Screen*. Westport: Praeger
Publishers.

Bradshaw, Peter (2018) James Bond of Film – OO7's best
and worst movies ranked! *The Guardian* [online]. Available
at https://www.theguardian.com/film/2018/aug/24/james-
bond-on-film-ranked [accessed 26 August 2018].

Broccoli, Albert, with Donald Zec (1998) *When the Snow
Melts*. London: Boxtree.

Calisi, Romano (1966) Myths and History in the Epic of
James Bond. In *The Bond Affair,* ed. Oreste Del Bueno &
Umberto Eco, translated by R. A. Downie. London:
MacDonald & Co.

Chapman, James (1999). *Licence to Thrill: A Cultural History of the James Bond Films*. London: I.B. Taurus.

Cork, John and Stutz, Collin (2007) *The James Bond Encyclopaedia*. London: Dorling Kindersley.

Del Bueno and Eco (1966) *The Bond Affair*. Translated by R. A. Downie. London: MacDonald & Co.

Eco, Umberto (1966) The Narrative Structure of Fleming. In *The Bond Affair*, ed. Oreste Del Bueno & Umberto Eco, translated by R. A. Downie. London: MacDonald & Co.

Ellis, John (1992) *Visible Fictions*. London: Routledge.

Field, Matthew & Chowdhury, Ajay (2015) *Some Kind of Hero: The Remarkable Story of the James Bond Films*. Stroud: The History Press.

Fischer, Saul (1979) The Spy Who Lived Twice. *Bondage*. Summer.

Fleming, Ian (1953) *Casino Royale*. London: Jonathan Cape.

Fleming, Ian (1954) *Live and Let Die*. London: Jonathan Cape.

Fleming, Ian (1960) *For Your Eyes Only*. London: Jonathan Cape.

Fleming, Ian (1964) *You Only Live Twice*. London: Jonathan Cape.

Fleming, Ian (1965) *The Man with the Golden Gun*. London: Jonathan Cape.

Fleming, Ian (1966) *Octopussy and The Living Daylights.* London: Jonathan Cape.

Glen, John (2001) *For My Eyes Only: My Life with James Bond.* London: B.T. Batsford.

Goldman, William (1996) *Adventures in the Screen Trade: A Personal View of Hollywood.* London: Abacus.

Harper, Kevin (1998) From the Archive: The Living Daylights. *OO7 Magazine.* 17, 44-45.

Hastings, Chris (2006) The OO7 flops who nearly killed Bond. *The Telegraph* [online] Available at https://www.telegraph.co.uk/news/uknews/1518941/The-007-flops-who-nearly-killed-Bond.html [accessed on 03 July 2018].

Hibben, Nina (1989) *The Making of Licence to Kill.* London: Hamlyn.

Kempley, Rita (1987) The Living Daylights. *The Washington Post* [online]. Available at https://www.washingtonpost.com/wp-srv/style/longterm/movies/videos/thelivingdaylightspgkempley_a09f96.htm??noredirect=on [accesed on 24 June 2018].

Krämer, Peter (1999) A Powerful Cinema-going Force? Hollywood and Female Audiences since the 1960s. In Stokes, M & Maltby, R. *Identifying Hollywood's Audiences: Cultural Identity and the Movies.* London: BFI.

Lisa, Philip and Pfeiffer, Lee (1992) *The Incredible World of OO7.* London: Boxtree.

Mather, Victoria (1986) The Living Daylights. *The Daily Telegraph*. June.

Meslow, Scott (2014) Timothy Dalton opens up about *Penny Dreadful*, leaving James Bond, and the demon in all of us. *The Week* [online]. Available from http://theweek.com/articles/447045/timothy-dalton-opens-about-penny-dreadful-leaving-james-bond-demon-all [accessed 21 June 2018].

Neale, Steve (2000) *Genre and Hollywood*. London: Routledge

O'Brien, Harvey (2012) *Action Movies: The Cinema of Striking Back*. New York: Wallflower Press.

Parshall, Peter F. (1991) Die Hard and the American Mythos. *The Journal of Popular Film and Television*, 18 (4), 135-144.

Pfeil, Fred (1995) *White Guys: Studies in Postmodern Domination and Difference*. London: Verso.

Queenan, Joe (2001) You Only Star Twice. *Hotdog*. Issue 13, July, p52.

Rebello, Steven (1989) The Ad Campaign that Wasn't. *Premier*. July, 15.

Sellars, Robert (2008) *The Battle for Bond*. Sheffield: Tomahawk Press.

Sobchack, Thomas (1988) The Adventure Film. In Gehring, W.D. *Handbook of American Film Genres*. Westport: Greenwood Press.

Tasker, Yvonne (1993) *Spectacular Bodies: Gender, Genre and the Action Cinema.* London: Routledge.

Westbrook, Caroline (1995) Ah, We've Been Expecting You, Mr Bond. *Empire,* 78, 86-96.

The World of James Bond: A Tribute to Cubby Broccoli [Television]. Broadcast ITV, 18 August 1996.

INDEX

ABOUT THE AUTHOR

Cary Edwards has been lecturing in Film Studies since 2005. Having developed an unhealthy love of cinema during childhood he transferred this into the academic world by completing the MA Film Studies at The University of East Anglia in 2002 and then a PhD from the Lincoln School of Film and Media, University of Lincoln. He has written for *Bright Lights Film Journal* and *Horror Homeroom,* spoken at film conferences and blogs at www.cary-edwards.com. *He Disagreed with Something that Ate Him* is his first book.

During his obsession with James Bond he entered, and won, a competition to be digitised into Activision's James Bond game *007 Legends,* for the Playstation 3 and X-Box 360. He appears as a Drax Henchmen in the *Moonraker* level (pictured above) and as a multiplayer character where he can be killed many, many, times.

Made in the USA
Middletown, DE
30 April 2021

38768685R00066